MAXIME COTON

In 2004, at the age of 18, his first collection of poetry, entitled *La Biographie de Morgane Eldä*, was published by Tétras Lyre.

Since then, in addition to numerous collaborations in magazines, he has published several books of poetry. He also develops other forms of writing (short stories, songs, theater plays).

Over the last years, Maxime Coton has been in increasing demand for poetry readings and performances in Belgium and France. In 2011 he founded Canopée, a band that mixes jazz, rock and poetry.

In order to fulfill his desire to put his energy at the service of other voices as much as his own, Coton became editor of the editions Tétras Lyre from 2009 to 2014. He launched a new collection, combining music and poetry, bringing the publishing house into the digital age.

He is relentlessly experimenting with crossovers between literature and digital media. His latest attempt to date is *Living Pages*, a Virtual Reality Poem, co-created with Paula Kehoe.

As a filmmaker, he has directed documentaries and experimental films.

The
Common
Gesture

Original title
Le Geste ordinaire
© 2011 by Esperluète Éditions

English translation
© 2017 by Bruits
info@bruitsasbl.be
http://www.bruitsasbl.be
ISBN: 978-2-930828-01-5

Layout & typesetting
Sébastien Vellut – lautobus.be

The Common Gesture

Maxime Coton

POEMS
translated from the French
by Nathaniel Rudavsky-Brody

Bruits

Slow is the time I take to reach you
The trains are always late
Before we arrive in the city
Here is the wall
Endless, unending, at an end
Enclosure of grime
Of nourishment the factory

I go to find you
Outside, the day when perhaps
Your face will be changed
And the town I was raised in
But no, in its sprawl its growth
The guard will not let us enter
My father (is nothing)

Work
I cannot go see the writing of
Your hands
I try not to think about class struggle

Film without images, I promise nothing

Tags on the walls that hide you
What the retina cannot record
The hand can see, approach
Searching for a way out, turning in circles around
The entrance into the world
Demon of words or private property?
The poem will be your guilty conscience,
Hears the guard, and behind him
Managers, director, oblivion

A tongue held back cannot stay silent
Images made from this moment onward
Will never be innocent
They will carry the violence
Of the unspoken, of one who without a word
Has set himself in hatred against others

I try not to think of Marx
Whom I have not read
I try not to speak
The language of books you have not read
Yet you see them not without pride
On my walls
Do not call them tools of power
Avoid such thoughts
They are the way I reach you
And wooden creeds will never set them alight

A word is more than an image
It is its possibility and renunciation
What hides behind the poem
A sharp pen I use to measure
The pierced streets

I am simply trying to explain
To explain to you simply
The language that separates us
Binds us as well by way of the unexpressed

Your body's movements in space
Muffied echoes around you
The book not written
The film unseen
But always behind the eye
A persistence

Sometimes the lie is waiting for us
Its direct superior is silence
I confuse fatherhood with
Human resources
But always at evening
The lamp that goes out too soon
On our exhaustion
Will invoke the price of our defiance

Not letting the idea grow inside me
That existing somewhere
Else, in another
World without factories
Would give you something
Resembling a second birth

In the world of images
I am beyond the law, I go
Everywhere I hear
In every place the murmur
Of fair trade, one life is worth
Another: we know
The lie is theirs
And we are powerless against it

A cry
Yes a cry if we can
Go forward each in the other
Through the invisible, this separate love
And the cry like a kiss
On a wrist Infinite turning

Dare the idea that
You and I are worth more than a jack-of-all-trades
Less than nothing
The voiceless
Fallen silent, the weight of whose words
                    will never be equal to
The mindlessness of repeated gestures

You always told me
Intelligence was yours
You never said it came from you
From your pores but thinking about it
I say, our intelligence
That of being alive
Will one day save us I swear it,
Father

Did I need to learn to write before I could read
                     your palms? Your palms cracked
                            from cold and ignorance?
I listen.
They say: "You will be a fracture. The one who
                     begot you carries it in himself.
                     It will be your cry, and the name
                            you are given will be that
                                   of reconciliation."
So, father, your hand makes a fist
                     but it does not clench:
                            no fight is calling.
In my blindness, I understand.
You were born, unaware, a utopia's failure.

I understand this and many other things
                     because I can read and write.
                            Because I have been given
                                   the time to see.

Think

Pass

I never became the boss

Pass, think

Yet every day, I tell myself

Think, pass

That your desire, your reason for living

Resides perhaps

Pass, think

In me becoming one day

The one who gives order

I make small nothings
I make what does not sell
Wind of a dream of being elsewhere
Sometimes near you
I am your guilty conscience
Unearthed
What you could not be
I fled from
Like a nightmare for us both

I am your unexpected
Freedom

I make nothing
Then sell you
What I call grace
(in you a few pages?)

At times the revealed
Impression of not going far enough
In the exploration of things

A deficiency of class

The hand before
It writes hesitates
Between mind and bone

. . . As if I was writing
To bring you into the world myself this time

Is this indecent?

The I in your mouth

That will not cross the gates

Which the rasp of effort peoples nevertheless

With life

I speak of you

I speak *for* you

Is this indecent?

If we are merely others

What gives me the right to say I

When no one is you?

You work
I watch you working
This is my work, my gaze
My questions have no market value.
And yet, I give them form. I assemble them
from your gestures.
I do not live by my hands. Your hands
are what I see, draw and praise.

You are the invisible
But what could be more real
Than this hand on the hammer
Than this spark that exceeds our forgetting
Prolongs it?

Where there is a dream
You make preparations
Where there is a future
A sum of experience to be renewed
And in between, the blind wall
Private, intimate, personal
Leads to the wisdom of limits

Your life is no mystery
Enough for itself
A hand in shadow
A life in the shadows
And against this, close against it
I press the seal of doubt
May nothing change

You are no longer needed

You can remain absent

See the day

Its incandescence

That will understand your silence

Will know the price of blindness

It is from knowing too much that every day

You advance down this cold passageway

Broken back cesspool

And suddenly with all the violence of a spreader

Of a pinch roller, of a cage. . . you are

Outside

The time behind you

Must become history

Before you will answer the questions

That were never raised by my rebellion

At the *if* of smooth words you will calmly

                                place a hand

Your breath, full and white, over me

Abandoned to the day
You go to bed without light
With no tomorrow
Each day that passes
Is younger
And in your book
Your record of work, I read
The imprint of your body
On unmade sheets
Your bed unmade by the dawn
A word in the form of a question
To work or not
We return to the daily fare
Of earth, your daily paper
Is silent

You are in the strength of your age

Like a quiet screw-jack

I am still only a child

No one is growing inside me

As my insolence in you

Light soup and forced snacks

One day, you too will grow up

And where the branch is joined to the trunk

I will carve the initials of gratitude

All you have is a car
A driver's seat, your pride
And giving more than you receive
Is enough

(synonym of liberty, of complete mastery of space,
of a certain way of the world)

You pull up and plant elsewhere. Sure of where you come from, you keep quiet. To the point of forgetting. But most of all, you are the one who disappears. The place you come from lies fallow: you plant elsewhere. Trust in the wind. Say again the gesture you are, repeat. Nothing more. With nothing else. The wind is enough to change your breath. Do not forget. Do not forget yourself.

I want to approach you

With something other than words

I write you

As I would speak of a dead man

We cry

With stones, with fire for example

With noise

I want to approach you

Talking

Before you

I speak in your absence

In your absence

I speak of a wire

From slippers to steel

Describing you is to bury
Already
Is adding emptiness, its charms
To that little of you made up of
Successive gestures
Rubble of breath

Everything is simple, you work
You have money because you work
You live because you have money
Everything is simple, according to rule
I cannot buy your submission
I admire and despise you

I seek the simple image
The man who has no place in language

Breaking open your lunch bags
I see fingers, mouths
Sudden gestures grown calm
Sandwiches made the night before
Answer Italian coffee
(at every hour of the day)
Disappear into it
And the simple rebounding
Movement of the cup
Toward the mouth
Diverts you, institution of rest
From a purely economic existence

I watch the workman's knees

Handler, fitter, turner, caster, roller, stamper,
                    moulder, spinner, comber,
                              beamer, twister

Which of these doubts is you?

One man is worth another

Is a lie

The weight of a man is a color

Blue collar

White collar

But the lines in your hands will one day

Show up the lie

A worker does work
And you become mine
A poet waits

A worker does work
Two men dance
Anonymous over time
Past, passing, arrived

A worker does work
The one who sings
Knits what binds him, weaves
Sickle and seed

A man
A force of work

A body
A building of silence

A voice
Fallen silent, forgetful

There were no more Sundays
But there survived, tenacious
The hollow watchword
Of the unoccupied
Health-work-cleanliness
You had to rub out
What remained under the fingernails
That shame

Unbolt the door

See the worker again

Riveting

See the truth

At work

In him like yesterday

The dictionary says that a proletarian is one who has only his hands. What does the proletarian say? Why this silence? Why, in the factory, so much noise?

Work

Neural center of a prayer

Unique safe-conduct through desolation

And simultaneously the infinite

Certainty of being

Laborious

We cover our nakedness

In the end, when hatred
Solitude, isolation have passed
What is left of us?

Shaved
At the end of the night, of the book
What remains when we are washed clean?

I walk and see your back,
Formless, calm mass, growing distant

Come back, come back

And I will go on your grave
If my ashes know how to read

Working, living elsewhere as I have done
Have I left or am I only torn
From a place without history
From a disappearance as a point of origin
This world is divided but I want no other

When you die
My age will take root on the ruins of yours
I will draw a lunch box
A bike, grease stains
On your grave

Inheritor of a debt,
There will be nothing for me to add
To the slowness of the hearth